Just Two Wings

JUST
TWO WINGS

by Janet Ealon Givens

Illustrated by Susan Elayne Dodge

ATHENEUM 1984 NEW YORK

Library of Congress Cataloging in Publication Data

Givens, Janet E.   Just two wings.

1. Birds—Migration—Pictorial works—
Juvenile literature.   1. Dodge, Susan Elayne.   II. Title.
QL698.9.G53   1983   598.2'525   83-2710

Published simultaneously in Canada by
McClelland & Stewart, Ltd.
Composition by Dix Type, Syracuse, N.Y.
Printed and bound by Halliday Lithograph Corporation, Inc.
West Hanover, Massachusetts
Typography by Mary Ahern
First Edition

A mysterious cloud moved
across the morning sky.
Closer and closer it came.

It broke into small black dots
that moved faster and faster.
Overhead the dots turned into birds,
and a thousand wings beat the air.

On they flew through clouds chased by a
   cold north wind.
Small leaves, still clinging to a
   cold bare branch,
      fluttered and waved good-bye.

WHERE ARE ALL THE BIRDS GOING?
These birds may be flying south
    in search of food.
Here the ground is frozen, and insects
    sleep in unknown places.

They must find a place where it is warmer—
where trees are green with leaves,
where plants flower to make seeds,
and where worms still wiggle
through soft brown earth.

BUT HOW CAN THEY FLY TO THESE
FARAWAY PLACES?
Sometimes they soar with a gentle wind.
Sometimes they ride on a current of air.

But when the air is still and no wind is blowing,
   they must make their wings beat the air
      again and again.
These almost weightless feathered wings
   with hollow bones
      can keep them high and move them
         on and on.

Birds get ready for these trips
  by eating well before they start.
Some of the food turns to fat beneath their
  thin, loose skin.
Some strengthens the muscles used to keep
  their wings moving up and down.

HOW CAN BIRDS FIND
   THESE FARAWAY PLACES?
Some scientists think they follow
   rivers and coasts,
      because they make long flights over land.
But what about birds who fly over oceans?

Some think these birds are born knowing
    the direction,
while others believe they use the sun and
    stars to help them find their way.

But no one knows for certain.
It is still a mystery!

Birds leave their nests to fly long
distances for many reasons.
Some search for places that have
more food,
but others want a place
with fewer birds
to share the food.

Still others like places where the sun shines
    longer
And days are warmer,
    and there is no need to fluff their feathers
    and hide against the wind.

And some birds stay where they are all winter.
They huddle together in sheltered places
to help them keep warm.

When we give them seeds they thank us
with their cheerful sounds.

DO THE SAME BIRDS COME BACK?
Some birds return to the same place
on the same day, year after year.

Some birds can even find the very same tree
with last year's nest waiting in the branches.

Most birds that fly south
   return to the same land when winter
gives way to spring.

For many years, people all over the world
have been trying to find out just where
    each kind of bird goes.
They put tiny bands with numbers
    on their legs to help keep track
        of their travels.

This is how
   we found out
that the Arctic Tern
   travels twenty-two
     thousand
     miles a year!
(This is almost as much
   as an entire trip
     around the world!)
They nest in the arctic north
   in the season when
     the sun never sets
and enjoy these light-filled days
   for three full months.

When the earth begins to tilt the other way, days grow shorter and these birds begin to migrate south.

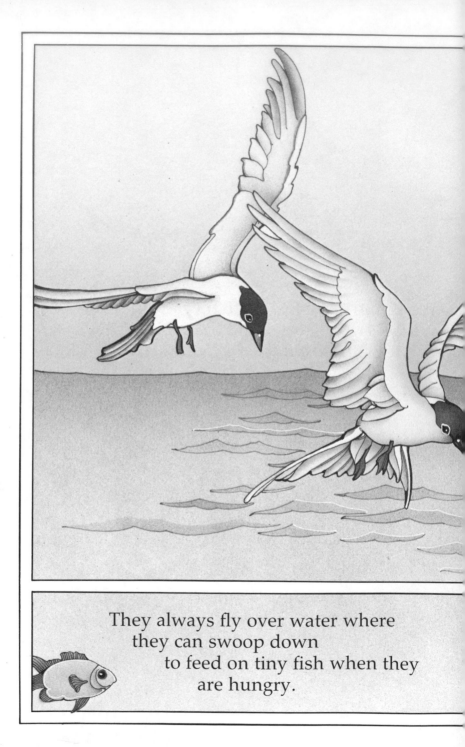

They always fly over water where
they can swoop down
to feed on tiny fish when they
are hungry.

By the time they reach the other end of the earth, it is the season there when the sun never sets, so once again they enjoy another three light-filled months!

HOW DO BIRDS KNOW WHEN TO RETURN?
Perhaps they just KNOW what to do
and when and how to do it.
This is called instinct.

Or perhaps they see new shadows fall
  or feel meadows warm beneath the strong
   spring sun,
or they see buds swell on boughs lacing
 a pale blue sky—

Something tells them it is time to go,
   the way a hot sticky summer's day
tells us it is time to go swimming again.

We know so many things about how
   birds migrate,
      but there are even more things
         we do not know.
We must keep asking questions and
   trying to find answers.

Then perhaps someday
we may really know
why and how birds
travel so far
on just two wings!